The Art of Relationship-ing™

New Strategies to Connect & Collaborate

by Laurie Grace Bouldin

Riley Smiley Publishing
Dallas, Texas

Copyright © 2012 Laurie Grace Bouldin

No part of this book may be used or reproduced in any manner without express written permission, excepting brief quotations embodied in articles and reviews.

For information about bulk purchases,
visit www.LaurieGraceBouldin.com

Published by Riley Smiley Publishing, Dallas, Texas

Cover photos by Kelly Rucker, www.KellyRucker.com
Edited by Deb Johnson, www.SpikeCommunications.com
Typing by Bonnie Nadine Newman, www.TypingTornado.Jimdo.com
Book design by Matt Mitchell, www.MattMitchellDesign.com
Illustrations by Darlene Mendez, Designs by Darlene

First Edition, Printed in the USA

ISBN: 978-0-9857878-0-6

We can create special books, booklets and excerpts from *The Art of Relationship-ing* suited for your group's needs. We can also customize training programs based on the content of this book.

For information, contact Laurie Grace Bouldin at
www.LaurieGraceBouldin.com.

For my husband, Patrick –
the love of my life
who taught me about
pop-up campers, bluegrass music
and true Partnership

Table of Contents

Acknowledgements vii
Introduction xi

1 You: The Common Denominator 1

2 The New Equation 9

3 Trust is the Foundation 17
   Where are You on the Trust Spectrum? 20
   See – Believe – Own 24
   Repair and Restore Damaged Trust 29
   Maintain Trust 33

4 The Brainy Truth 39
   Get in on the Ground Floor 49
   Tap into the "Ka-POW" 53
   Brainflash: Smart Relationship-ers Maneuver Finicky Brains 59
   Make a Difference by Making a Change 66

5 Gender Smarter 71
   Part I: He-focus and She-focus 79
   Part II: Meet Mr. Provider and Ms. Connector 92
   Part III: Men of Actions and Women of Words 99
   Part IV: The Deal with "I'm Sorry" 105
   Part V: Commit to a BIG Give 112
   How the New Equation all Comes Together 113

6 It's a...Partnership! 115
   The Big Shift 119
   WOW! Factor 122
   It All Starts with You 125

Afterword: The Rest of the Story 129
About the Author 134

Acknowledgements and Appreciation

Mom – You gave me life and love – and still do. Thank you for being there for me, *always*. I proclaim you as the Queen of prayer. How blessed I am to have you as my Mom.

Nana and Papa – My heart of gratitude feels unending appreciation and love for you. Nana, you have given me a lifetime of confidence; Papa, you have filled me with fatherly love. I'm a lucky girl.

Patrick – We did it. Together we created this book! Your support and encouragement provided the fuel I needed to keep going. You *are* my hero – forever.

Jonathan Cude – I am forever thankful for your encouragement and wisdom during such a transforming time in my life. It has brought me to where I am today.

40-Day Team – From prayer to proofreading, to typing, editing, illustrating and designing, YOU each were my partners in Collaborating to make this book come to life…in 40 days. Yes, the time line was crazy in human terms, but you believed in and supported me and my desire to do it on the timeline that God gave me. And, we all made it happen.

Deb Johnson – Wow, we did this together. You are the Editor Extraordinaire. Thank you for caring about this work and making it great.

Bonnie Nadine Newman – You truly are the Typing Tornado. As I was penning the book text, you were typing it. We make quite the team. Many thanks for your speedy work.

Darlene Mendez – Your hand-drawn illustrations gave this book that special touch I wanted. Thanks for your caring, diligent work ethic and amazing artistic talent.

Matt Mitchell – Yep, we did it (just like you said we could). Thanks for your always calm, "can do" attitude. Oh, and for the awesome cover design.

Niesha Alexander –Thank you for keeping track of all of the important details that enabled me to get moving with the book. Working with you is a joy, and I look forward to all that is ahead of us.

Extra special thanks – Mom, Nana, Patrick, Missy, Jacqueline, Lori, Christian, Bridgette, Lauren, Melanie and Mary… for all that you did and still do for me, xoxoxo.

Forty Five Ten – Missy and crew in the T Room, thanks for keeping me well fed during many hours of writing. The beautiful environment and smiles kept me in my zone.

Faith Boosters – Each day of this 40-day book-writing journey, I filled up and was sustained by words from your books: Rick Warren – *The Purpose Driven Life,* Bruce Wilkinson – *The Prayer of Jabez* and Eugene Peterson – *The Message.*

Acknowledgements and Appreciation

Rock-Solid Resources – Your work has been significant in my personal and professional transformation: Alison Armstrong (and the many workshop leaders) with PAX Programs, Scott Haltzman, M.D. and Author, John Gottman, Ph.D. and Author and David Rock and trainers at Results Coaching.

National Speakers Association, North Texas Chapter – Generosity and professionalism can and do mix, and this group exemplifies that. I am grateful to be part of your community.

>*Adele Good* –Thank you for telling me about NSA and inviting me to my first meeting.

>*Sally Baskey* – I am crazy about you! Special thanks for our collaboration on my title.

>*Karen Cortell Reisman* –You are great; I am so fortunate to have you as my NSA mentor.

>*Christine Cashen* – Because of our Corner Bakery visit together, this book happened! Thank you for your continued, spot-on advice (and for being my unofficial mentor, shhh).

>*Other NSA wiz kids* –Mary Warren, Tim Durkin, Stu Schlackman and Gary Rifkin – you have each been an inspiration to me in so many ways. I am blessed to know you.

Introduction

Relationships are our greatest assets.

They are the conduits that help you achieve any level of success that you'll ever have. Taking great care of them makes all the difference in the quality of our lives. Once I realized and began living into that truth, everything changed for me.

I began to see that having what I most wanted in life was dependent on the quality of my relationships. *The Art of Relationship-ing* was born out of my desire to achieve that.

There are things in life that are easy, and things in life that are hard. I advocate keeping the easy things easy because the hard things are hard enough.

Relationships don't have to be so hard. Yes, there is new possibility that you'll discover within this little book. It encompasses all of your relationships. Here, a new horizon appears. Hope is reestablished with a new pathway to how we relationship with others.

The Art of Relationship-ing

I've discovered a simpler, more fulfilling way to create relationships that WOW! and transform results. That's what I will be sharing with you.

With love and care, I've written with one goal in mind: to share information with you that is useful and will make a big difference for you in your relationships and ultimately in your life.

So, settle in with me here, and let's explore together. The good news is that this new approach is fun, creative and practical – and it leads to new results. Get ready to have your thinking stirred, your paradigms tilted and your perspectives transformed.

Let's grow together. It all begins with you, now.

With love and appreciation,

Laurie Grace Bouldin

Dallas, Texas

www.LaurieGraceBouldin.com

Introduction

> *My personal mission as an author*
> *is to write with wit, wisdom and heart,*
> *by God's hand.*
>
> *My mission and purpose for this work*
> *is to bring new possibility, ease and fulfillment*
> *to your life...one relationship at a time.*

Chapter 1

You: The Common Denominator

• •

"What lies behind us and lies before us are tiny matters compared to what lies within us."

– Ralph Waldo Emerson

Chapter 1 • You: The Common Denominator

You are the Common Denominator in each of your relationships; changing you has the power to transform every relationship you have.

I was married to my high school sweetheart for 17 years – and then we divorced. At that point, I reassessed everything in my life – relationships, career, outlook, faith, the whole shebang.

Relationships drew my attention. In my assessment, most of my relationships (especially those with men) rated somewhere between mediocre and dysfunctional. Ugh.

That's when I decided to take a snapshot of my landscape. I found that I was in every view. Yes, I was the Common Denominator amidst all the angst and dissatisfaction in my relationships. We each share this basic truth, whether we realize it or not. Once I was willing to see it for myself, everything changed.

Since I am a "glass half full" person, I saw something good in this. The glimmer of hope was in the possibility of changing me. I knew I had full control over my actions, reactions, responses and choices. With that, I could create something new and more intentional in me, and take it into every relationship going forward. So, if I wanted to change the results I was living with, I had to start by changing how I relationship-ed with others.

At once I was both excited and petrified. My choice was simple: stay right where I was and keep getting the same results, or do something different with the hope of getting a new and improved result.

It was like being at the eye doctor and hearing, "1 or 2, 2 or 1, 1 or 2..."

Feeling I had nothing to gain by keeping my current course, I chose to hit, "Reset." When I did, my new life started. I just didn't know it at that time.

The ripple effect started immediately. I tossed a stone into a new pond and the gentle rings of water began moving outward, from me.

Change was possible at the moment I said "yes." Without it, I was stuck. I was unwilling to keep getting what I didn't want. I was smarter than that. I had too much life still to live. I wanted to live with more joy, passion, intention and satisfaction – at work and at home.

That's when the "gulp" set in. I had committed to going for something new. This was a shift in me that would trickle into all of my relationships and magically transform them. Snap! Just like that!

What was I thinking? Yes, "gulp." I had a new taste in my mouth: risk mixed with vulnerability. It didn't taste good at all. Where did my happy, hopeful ideas about transforming relationships go? Reality set in, and I relearned that saying "yes," was just the first step. The next step meant getting clear on what I wanted, and then going for it.

Anytime you go for something new, nervousness is inevitable. For me, it felt like a tidal wave. But I am both a survivor and a believer. I was able to overcome the wave of anxiety and live into the belief of new possibility with my relationships. And I did.

Once I said, "yes," and took action to move forward in a new way, I started living with new results. Through personal and professional transformation, I Reset my world! While living into it, *The Art of Relationship-ing* was being born.

A sweet journey, looking back. The two lessons I learned in the early days of change are worth sharing:

Lesson 1

Be "eyes wide open" with your relationships

Knowing your truth is your starting point. Your reality is what it is. Think about stepping onto a scale. There's awareness in front of you, if you're willing to see it. It's worth the look.

So, think about some relationships that are important to you. Think broadly and creatively. Family, friends, colleagues, clients;

even relationships you don't have but would like to have. Don't fall prey to analysis paralysis on coming up with the "right" list. You can always come back and tweak it later.

Next, assign a grade to each relationship based on your results. There's no right or wrong on defining "results." That's up to you. So, write down a letter grade (A, B, C, D or F) beside each of your names. That's your starting point. This is where you take a long, hard look in the mirror.

It's important to see and consider exactly what's there. Are you *getting* what you want from these relationships? Are you *giving* what you really want to be giving? Are you *showing up* as the person you want to be? These questions are eye-openers and can be the launch of a new beginning in your relationships.

You've just looked at what exists currently in your relationships, and now it's time to move forward.

Lesson 2

Consider and choose what you want in and from your relationships

Figuring out your final destination is key. It's far too easy and commonplace to talk about what you don't want or don't like. This often shows up as nagging or complaining. But really, that never gets you where you want to go. Or at least not efficiently.

Chapter 1 • You: The Common Denominator

Instead, get really clear, and boldly choose what you want *in* and *from* your relationships.

Don't know where to start? Look back at the list of relationships you created earlier. What would you like each of those grades to be? It would be easy to say you would like each to be an "A." Right? Of course. But remember that this shift in grade is dependent on you and the changes and actions you are willing to make.

Consider what new grade you would like to work for, say, in the next three months. Now, write that grade beside each name and circle it.

So how do you get there? In the pages to come, you will learn skills and tools that will help you be more successful in your relationships, so you're getting the results you want.

It's true that you are only one part – 50% – of your relationships. But, you have the choice to be 100% committed to your 50%. My experience has shown me that when I show up with my 100% commitment, people begin responding to me differently. And, then, the relationship starts changing. And, *I* was the change agent.

Likewise, you can make changes in your life and in your relationships. So let's go, you incredible Common Denominator!

Chapter 2

The New Equation

"You have infinite possibilities in your life,
but they will be realized only when
you take action."

– Alexandra Stoddard

There's a profound New Equation for creating and recreating relationships; it will enable you to have greater simplicity, satisfaction and productivity – by taking a whole new approach.

Take one Common Denominator and blend with Science and Soul to get more satisfying and WOW!-ing relationships at work and at home. This is the New Equation that will rock your world! It sets the stage for getting more goodies from your relationships with greater ease.

No, this isn't snake oil nor is it "turn that frown upside down," positive thinking. This is a new, smart way to create and connect with others. Like the iPod created a new way to listen to music, this new relationship equation creates a new way to access and experience the many people in your life.

Chapter 2 • The New Equation

Science? Yes. Brain Science. Learning how our brains receive, process and then respond to others will blow your mind! With this knowledge, you will see all the ways you can make tweaks and changes that yield big differences – huge differences!

What's terrific is how simple many of the changes are. As a Queen Maximizer and credentialed coach, I am committed to providing you with new tips and tools that will enable you to go from "good" to "great" with ease and efficiency.

Get ready to be stretched and have your thinking stirred and spurred. Remember, *The Art of Relationship-ing* is about creating new possibilities. This starts by giving you new information which creates the space for you to have new awareness. That's when things get fun and you start moving in new directions!

You'll become the pro at leading conversations that result in Connection and Collaboration instead of confusion and frustration. With some Brain Science, you will show up ready, willing and able to inspire and expand others. It will be like money in the bank, equipping you with a treasure chest of jewels to share with others, via your words to them.

These jewels are rarely used in our everyday workplaces, board meetings, homes and schools. They are undiscovered by many.

But smart reader, you will have these valuable treasures at your fingertips.

Soul? I'm talking about your humanity, your person, your heart. This ushers in your individuality, sincerity and vision! Science explains brain wiring and Soul adds heart and feeling to the mix. Soul makes it real and worth going for.

We are emotional beings, and we must factor this reality into our relationship equation. Without it, there are only systematic robotic activities and occurrences, not relationships. The movie, "Stepford Wives" comes to mind.

I once worked with a man whose actions and demands invited our heads to work, but not our hearts. Sadly, he missed out on excellent results from the team because of our limited and censored existence. I see corporate America waking up to this reality, finally but slowly.

As you pair Science and Soul at home and at work, you can be the innovator. Here's the fun: you can be like a secret agent as you implement these new and simplified techniques. No one has to know what you're up to. No walking in one day proclaiming, "I've come to bring Science and Soul to this meeting!" Shhh! Be undercover about this mission. People will begin noticing how different the results are when you're present.

Chapter 2 • The New Equation

In an instant, you may be thought of as a communication and relationship rock star! Get ready.

Here's the catch: you must bring an open mind to this new, unique approach to relationships. Only you can choose to do that. Will you? Resistance to change is normal, but your choice to make change can prevail.

In the pages to come, you will discover new ways to relationship with others; the information is validated; it works. It will make a difference for you and the people in your lives. You'll see.

So let's make a deal. If you will approach the information in this book with focus and an open and willing mind, I commit that you'll discover several nuggets big enough to WOW! your relationship results!

Here's the overview of where the following pages will take you:

- Trust – it's the foundation of your relationships. You'll assess the condition of your foundation and learn how to repair and maintain it. With a good Trust foundation in your relationships, you're ready to start building upon them.

- Brainy Truths – these tips and tools help you better connect with others…brain-to-brain. You'll learn how to simplify your conversations while inspiring and motivating others. And, you'll see the benefits and learn the "how to" of becoming a true Connector – one conversation at a time.

- Gender Smarter – you will have new awareness of the fundamental, innate differences in the sexes. You'll learn each sex's instinctive drivers and strengths so you can maximize your collaborative efforts – regardless of gender.

- Partnership – it's the final destination – the cream of the crop in relationships. Piecing together Trust with Brainy Truths and Gender Smarts gets you here. The WOW! results you most want are only possible through Partnership. You'll learn that contribution is what makes those WOW! results happen.

Now it's time to learn about the foundational principle that all great relationships have in common: Trust.

Chapter 2 • The New Equation

Chapter 3

Trust is the Foundation

"…the search for outward simplicity,
for inner integrity, for fuller relationship…"

– Anne Morrow Lindbergh

Great Trust is required for great relationships. Trust comes first. Always. It is the Ace of Spades and trumps everything else.

What is Trust?

How you see and define Trust defines the foundation of your relationships. Webster defines it as, "dependence or reliance on the character, ability, strength or truth of someone or something." Dictionary.com brings in "integrity and surety." How do you define Trust?

When you have Trust, you have confidence. Without it, you have fear that dresses up as uncertainty, hesitance and guardedness. A modified, lesser version of self appears with broken Trust.

Have you seen that to be true of yourself? In others? It is exhausting and limiting. Sigh.

Let's flip our thinking. Consider a relationship you have that has great Trust. Take a pause here to think about this, and get a picture of that person in your mind. Okay – got it?

How would you describe that relationship? Who are you in that relationship? What makes it so great? What does that relationship create or produce? All of that paints a beautiful picture of Trust as you know and experience it.

What's in it for You?

Confidence and comfort are resident in Trusting relationships. Wouldn't it be incredible if you could establish more of this? Trust opens new doors to simplicity and possibility – like walking into a conversation with ease instead of on eggshells.

What is Possible with Trust?

Reliance, dependence and confidence flow freely in Trusting relationships. And, they put the welcome sign out for individual expression, creativity and motivation in others. Now we're talking! What employer, leader, team member or friend wouldn't want all that?

Where are You on the Trust Spectrum?

Understanding your relationships begins with an initial assessment – your own inspection report of your Trust foundation.

Chapter 3 • Trust is the Foundation

In successful Relationship-ing, it's essential that you have this information before making any relationship decisions or changes. These two questions will help you assess where you are on the Trust spectrum:

- How well do *you* Trust others?

- How well do *others* Trust you?

Think broadly about your answers to gain a holistic view of where you are. Now, let's place a magnifying glass over this and take another view.

Create a list of the 10 people you have the most frequent contact with right now. Family, friends and coworkers should be present on your list. Now ask yourself the two Trust questions above about each of your 10 people, and fill in your list with letter grades.

The second question will be based on your perception unless you've received feedback directly from that person.

Here's an example of my list:

Trust Grades –		
10 people who I am in contact with most frequently		
Name	I trust them	They trust me
Paul	A	A
Sharla	B	B
Brenda	A	A
Connie	B	A
Dee	C	B
Lou	A	A
Andy	B	B
Kara	A	A
Billy	B	B
Jacob	B	B

What's key in this exercise is that you spend some time to pause, consider and reflect. When you are willing to look deeply into something, it's amazing what you can see and learn.

What are some initial insights you are having about Trust in your various relationships? How do you feel about your grades?

My list revealed that I spend the most time with people whom I really trust. I feel encouraged and safe being with them.

Chapter 3 • Trust is the Foundation

The previous exercise included your primary relationships – those people with whom you have frequent contact. Now, do the same exercise with five people who are VIPs in your life but didn't show up on your first list.

Here's an example of my list:

Trust Grades – top 5 VIPs not on the earlier list		
Name	I trust them	They trust me
Katy	B	B
SarahBeth	C	B
Tom	B	B
Jim	B	B
Aaron	C	B

What are you noticing with this list? What prevented these people from being on your first list? What do you think about what you're seeing?

The standout for me was that my Trust grades were lower on my second list. Ugh, and the second list captured five of my VIPs! These lower scores illustrate that when the Trust foundation isn't solid, it doesn't feel safe. And, when you don't feel safe in relationships, you tend to give them less time, energy and effort.

Just like a home inspector writes a report to a potential home buyer indicating the current condition of a house, you're creating a Trust inspection report for yourself that gives you indications of where trouble spots are and could be. It also lets you know where things are working well.

See – Believe – Own

It's not about them – it's about you.

Relationships may be a two-way street, but this book is written just for you (and not for all of the people you know who you wish were reading it). You must take personal responsibility as the Common Denominator of your relationships. Once you do, amazing things can happen. I know; they did for me.

I went through this Seeing, Believing, Owning experience when I realized I was the Common Denominator in all of my less-than-stellar relationships years ago.

Once I was willing to see the truth about Trust in my relationships, I was able to shift my focus and see things from the ground up. You can, too. You'll learn that getting Trust right enables everything else. So naturally, it's the smart place to start.

Now, it's time to really 'take on' your Trust starting point – by Seeing, Believing, and Owning those Trust grades from the lists you made earlier.

Step 1 – *See* Your Starting Point

Whether you're at a professional football game, at a bird preserve or in a cooking class, you want to get a zoomed-in view of exactly what's going on. You look at the jumbo screen, pick up a pair of binoculars or walk to the kitchen to get close to the action. You want to see with your eyes.

As you gain this up-close view, you can assess the situation more clearly and accurately. Without this view, your awareness and experience are diminished.

But, sometimes looking at something up-close is unpleasant. Nonetheless, it's necessary. It is what it is, so you might as well look at it. Years ago, that was me. And, that aha moment allowed me to get a panoramic view like never before – my reality hit me in a snap. I began seeing with new eyes.

Seeing like this is the beginning of change. You move from the mindset of "yeah, yeah, I know, I know" to "oh, wow, I see that now."

In the earlier section, you started looking into the condition of Trust in your relationships. You're now seeing what's there. The lists of grades are now in your view.

Now stretch and take another action step towards *Seeing* in your daily life.

Here's your new assignment: become an observer.

Begin looking, listening and observing with zoomed-in awareness and notice what's new for you to see about Trust in your relationships. Becoming more observant will heighten your focus. And, with focus, you see reality more clearly and begin to take action.

Once I chose to see myself as the Common Denominator of my struggling relationships, I began seeing it more and more. My eyes were opened anew. How didn't I see it before?

Seeing is a where the journey begins. Believing comes next.

Step 2 - *Believe* What You See Is Real

You see and become aware of things with your *eyes*. You did this in Step 1.

Chapter 3 • Trust is the Foundation

You *believe* and acknowledge things with your *heart*. It's here that the truth of your starting point really soaks in. And, it needs to soak in.

As I began *truly* seeing my new reality, I was struck by the impact of it all. The realization moved from my eyes into my heart. I began *believing*. The dots were connecting – from me, to my relationships, to the quality of my life personally and professionally.

Further acknowledging where you are with Trust is the point in Step 2. When you allow this understanding to get into your heart, it becomes part of you. Consider these questions to gain an even greater perspective:

- What stories could be told by others about how you demonstrate and create Trust?

- What examples do you have that illustrate your Trust in others?

You've now seen and believed the current condition of your Trust. It's time to own it – that's the next step.

Step 3 - *Own* Your Situation

The blindfold is off. You see the number on the scale. You're beginning to connect your own dots.

In the previous sections, you made your lists, gave yourself grades and answered various questions about Trust. The reality of where you are on the Trust spectrum is here; it's clear.

Now it's time to *Own* it.

You've seen the truth with your eyes and believed it and placed it in your heart. Moving it into your head is what *Owning* it is about.

My relationship Reset from years ago happened once I began *Owning* my truth. It moved from my eyes, into my heart, and then into my head. That's where my logical mind powered on, and I thought, "This is mine. It's about me. It's not about them. I am 100% in control of my commitment and my *give* to my relationships." Upon Owning all of that, I began moving forward and changing my life...one relationship at a time.

You choose what you *Own*. Will you choose to *Own* where you are on the Trust spectrum now?

Remember, this is about you, no one else. Once you *Own* your Trust starting point, and take it on as yours, you can take action

– change it, fix it, make it better, keep it great. And, that's what the following two sections are about. Read on.

Repair and Restore Damaged Trust

Take action and fix damaged Trust. Get it right and make it better – it's essential. Now.

When Trust is damaged, you can either move to fix it or ignore it. There is really only one option if you want to have abundant relationships: repair and restore the damage.

Not sure what damaged Trust looks like? See the next table for some telltale signs.

Signs that Trust Could Be Broken or Damaged:
• People are less engaged and more tentative with you than you see them being with others.
• Your conversations are limited and lack the free flow of ideas, thoughts and opinions.
• Your conversations are more like monologues than dialogues.
• You don't really know the people around you – what's important to them, who they really are.
• Laughter and creative expression from others rarely surface in your presence.

Damaged Trust shows up in a variety of ways. But, here's what is key to know about it: Trust is damaged when someone is hurt.

And, when someone is hurt, healing is what's needed. It is the remedy. This basic truth is something children are taught from an early age. It applies to damaged Trust as well.

Here's what it all comes down to:

> ***Authentic* Apologies Heal People**
>
> **and**
>
> **Healed People are Able to Trust**

This applies to work relationships as much as to personal relationships.

Apologies are direct, action-based, for a purpose and enabling. Unfortunately, because pride often gets in the way, too few apologies occur. But, apologies are just as effective for adults as they are for children. Perhaps hearing a parent figure in your ear – "now apologize for that" – would be a good thing.

Reflect on the next table – what an apology is and what it does.

An Apology is ...
expressing regret and requesting forgiveness.
As Rick Warren explains in his book, *The Purpose Driven Life*, an apology is the fundamental key to restoring a relationship because it makes *the person* more important than the problem.
In making a sincere apology, pride is put aside. This demonstrates humility and builds bridges. Walls come down.

Here are the essential ingredients to giving an apology that heals and restores Trust:

1. You must be *authentic* and *sincere.*

2. You must take ownership. It sounds like this: "I am sorry that I ____" (fill in the blank). You are sincerely apologizing for *what was real to the other person* even when you don't fully agree with or understand the hurt. This requires a big dose of generosity. Note: an apology given *this way is* the restoring agent.

3. Keep your purpose in mind. The objective is to restore Trust, which is foundational to having a great relationship.

4. Be patient. Your apology enables the other person to flip the Trust switch back "on." But just like starting a car on a cold winter day, it takes some time for it to warm-up. Not a long time, but some time.

Do you see that damaged Trust is the problem and that the apology is the action that solves the problem?

You can't solve a problem if you aren't aware you have one, and that's why all of the previous sections in this chapter are so essential. You can't tap into the magical powers of apologies if you're not clear on what or where your problems are – and only you can assess that.

Once I really *owned* the truth of my relationship havoc, I began taking action. I couldn't not. *Owning* allowed me to see the problem. Then, I took responsibility for it and its resolution. Yes, I was fueled to move with my eyes, heart and head to the truth of my starting point. Because of that, my action was well placed, and I began relationship-ing with others in a simpler, more fulfilling way.

You're now equipped to do that same thing and focus on the foundational component of every relationship – Trust. Yes, it's time to take action.

Once you've used these tools to fix what's broken, then you can shift your attention to keeping the Trust in your relationships in good working order. Read on to learn how you can do just that.

Maintain Trust

Keeping an eye on your relationships and being intentional in taking care of them is smart and effective. Maintaining Trust is easier than repairing it, so focus on keeping your relationships intact.

Just as you maintain your home, your car and your body, good relationships also require maintenance. This starts with keeping close to Trust. You already have a commitment to the concept of preventive maintenance. Think about an oil change or a semi-annual visit to your dentist's office. You believe in the value of what those actions will prevent.

The Art of Relationship-ing

Relationships are your greatest assets. They are the conduits that help you achieve any level of success you'll ever have. Taking good care of them means maintaining them. This is often described as having "pride in ownership." Let's take pride in our relationships and give them the care and upkeep they deserve.

Maintaining Trust in relationships prevents their decay. The opposite of maintaining is ignoring or neglecting. There is no middle ground; you're doing one or the other. The choice is yours to make.

With automobile maintenance, it's common to think about these things:

1. What's recommended?

2. What's required?

3. How much will it cost?

4. How often do you schedule it?

5. What are the benefits?

Now shift gears and think about how these same questions apply to "Trust" maintenance.

The Trust Builders in the next table are great starting points for expanding and further building Trust in your relationships.

These three qualities add fuel to the Trust and Partnership tanks like you wouldn't believe! You can never give enough of each of these to the people around you. They inspire and motivate. They produce a kind of 'self-fuel' in others. And, when people have fuel of their own, you're not having to constantly "fill them up." Use them genuinely – everyone will benefit!

Trust Builders
• Appreciation – of what someone has said or done (it's the 'thank you')
• Acknowledgement – of someone's courage, actions, efforts, ideas or character (it's the 'look at you')
• Affirmation – of someone's progress, commitment or learning (it's the 'way to go')

Expressing appreciation inspires others to keep going and giving. Acknowledgement provides a confidence boost that fuels an individual to think more broadly and deeply in exploring additional ways to contribute. Affirming communicates more than approval – it focuses on accomplishment and progress. It delivers congratulations and kudos that provide inspiration to keep things moving in the current direction.

What does it cost you? A little time mixed with sincerity, belief and commitment.

Are the results worth it? Heck yeah – give it a try! Begin mindfully and sincerely practicing and fueling others with this trio. You will see new results in your Connections with others – increased motivation and improved morale.

Chapter 3 • Trust is the Foundation

With Trust in check, you will have a great foundation for your relationships. Now, let's build upon that. In the next chapter, you'll learn new, simplified ways of better connecting in your relationships – while keeping the brain in mind.

Chapter 4

The Brainy Truth

"Kindness in words creates confidence and kindness in thinking creates profoundness…"

– Lao Tzu

The Art of Relationship-ing

Becoming aware of Brain Science reveals new ways you can connect and create with others – without forcing, demanding or controlling.

Knowing a little Brain Science will make a world of difference in your relationships. Why? Brains are like picky eaters. They are finicky – they like what they like. As a result, the more you know about the brains likes, dislikes and preferences, the easier you can create the kinds of conversations you need and want to have.

Can you think back to a recent conversation that went all wrong? It's likely that once you were knee-deep into the downward spiral, you started thinking, "How in the world did we get here?" Then the next thought may have been, "How the heck do we get out of this mess?"

We've all been there too many times. The messy conversation leaves us feeling irritated, frustrated, confused and possibly angry. And now we have to focus on repairing things. Ugh!

Would you like to trade that in for another way? (Please say yes).

This new way of connecting brain-to-brain simplifies and improves the outcomes of those conversations profoundly.

Chapter 4 • The Brainy Truth

The truth and practice of all of this plopped into my life when I began training to become a credentialed coach years ago. Before that, I knew nothing about neuroscience and how it could give me a whole new quality of life, one conversation at a time.

Looking back I think, "What would my conversations be like without this knowledge?" I smile and shake my head. I know what they would be like: frequent tense and frustrating conversations that were too long and left me without what I wanted. I would have conversations that were over before they even began. Can you relate?

In this chapter, you will get a dose of Brain Science that is seemingly simple yet deeply impactful. You will not walk away a neuroscience guru; instead, you will dance away with new possibility about how to create terrific conversations and interactions that lead you to the outcomes you want. Yes, really!

It begins with you – giving up controlling and directing conversations. Why? Because this approach short circuits connection every time. Instead, you'll learn how to ask questions and listen in a way that makes a significant difference in the quality and depth of your relationships. With this strategy, you are guaranteed to have fewer messy conversations.

Connect and Collaborate

Becoming a Connector and Collaborator in your relationships is where great things begin to happen.

Take a glance at the information below and see if you fit into either category. Room to grow? Well, Brain Science will help you make that happen. Keep reading.

Do These Words Describe You?	
You might be a Connector if you…	You might be a Collaborator if you and others…
Attach	Cooperate
Join	Work together
Link	Join forces
Unite	Team-up
Associate	Work in partnership
Bond	Pool resources

Why is Connecting and Collaborating so Important?

Because it's a more efficient and productive way to work together, and it keeps the brain in mind. This approach is exactly the opposite of how we naturally interact with others, but the results are well worth the shift. The result? You will begin having amazingly simple and meaningful conversations – a win for you!

Chapter 4 • The Brainy Truth

In addition, the person you're having a great conversation with wins because you will be honoring and expanding that person by opening and inviting that person's brain to the conversation – who will in turn think time with you is inspiring and motivating. As a result, everyone impacted by these new conversations wins. Think about how far the ripple effect can go here. These results are far reaching and powerful.

You will become distinctive because you are creating new connections that are robust in generosity and alluring in how they bring out the best in others. People may begin to think you have some kind of magic dust that you sprinkle on them. They will feel honored, valuable and greater after being in your presence. Really!

It's because you will be asking them questions and talking to them in ways that cause them to think, to consider, to ponder and to reflect.

Refer to the Delightful Dozen questions. Each is intended to inspire thinking. You'll notice that they don't focus on details. As you master the Brainy Truths, you'll learn how unimportant details are when trying to support someone in creating an idea or solution. Counter-intuitive? Yes, but this is how the brain works.

Give these questions a try. Here's how: the next time you're talking to someone and discussing a problem or dilemma, jump in with these questions (instead of your advice, direction and ideas). These questions are intended to spur thinking. It often takes as many as five questions for things to get moving in the brain, so don't give up too early!

Chapter 4 • The Brainy Truth

Delightful Dozen –
questions to stir your thinker and someone else's

1. How much has this been on your mind?
2. On a scale of 1 to 10, how important is this to you?
3. What priority is this for you right now?
4. What priority do you want it to be?
5. How motivated are you to resolve this issue?
6. How clear are you about it?
7. Can you see any gaps in your thinking?
8. How do you feel about the resources you've put into this so far?
9. Do you have a plan for shifting this issue?
10. What are you noticing about your thinking?
11. How might you think about this differently?
12. How can I best help you further?

These Delightful Dozen questions may be a radical shift in your approach. With them, you will stop being the kings and queens of dishing out orders, opinions and advice. This may seem uncomfortable at first; change always is. But, stretch, shift and explore this new way of Connecting brain-to-brain – experience the benefits for yourself.

Unfortunately, this wasn't the case with my colleague.

The Art of Relationship-ing

A couple of weeks ago, I met her for breakfast. I was asking her advice on some business ideas, and I let her know upfront what I was most needing from our time together.

We were off to a great start – for the first two minutes! But from minutes 3 to 60 – geesh – my brain was registering threat signals one after another. Rather than listening and drawing me out, she was telling me what to do, explaining how I could've done things better, etc., etc. Threat signals cause the brain to switch from receive mode to reject mode. And, *my* brain was in full-blown reject mode.

She had no idea what was happening. Me, with my finicky brain, sat there hearing her voice – but I had tuned out – completely! And so it was – she wasted her words and together we wasted time and energy on a conversation that went nowhere.

But it doesn't have to be that way for you.

For starters, you now have the Delightful Dozen questions to get you moving in a new direction right away. Wonderful – now, let's add to it.

Terrific Listening Makes all the Difference

In order to be a great Connector, you have to be a fabulous listener. Dynamic Duo Listening will make all the difference for you. It's important to know what someone values, needs and wants if you really want to Connect. These new keys to listening will enable you to get to the heart of the matter more quickly when talking with someone. There, you will gain more from your conversations and negotiations in less time.

Dynamic Duo Listening
Key #1 - Listen for the emotion.
Key #2 - Listen for the repeat.

Emotion?

Yes. We are emotional beings who make decisions and take action based on knowledge. Sure, our logical minds help us process information and convert it to knowledge. But once we have knowledge, it is our emotions that trigger our action or inaction.

Focus keenly on listening for emotion in your interactions. Once you hear it and see it, attend to it, because that's what is important to the person right in front of you. No guessing required. Address what is real and present. It's quick, simple, respectful and generous.

Repeat?

Yes. We repeat what's important to us. Interestingly, the person who is doing the repeating typically is unaware of doing so. The smart listener knows about this and hones in on it quickly. Once you hear something a couple of times, ask the repeat-er about it. The other person thinks you're brilliant and insightful in knowing what is most important. It's terrific for both of you and happens because you smartly listened.

There are lots more Brainy Truths in the pages to come that will bring new possibility and change for you. I will be serving up various options. You pick and choose what works for you, and what feels like "you." Then you'll make this all your own. And of course, you'll write me and tell me all about the difference it is making in your relationships!

Now, let's move a step further into these Brainy Truths. In the next section, you'll see what you always want to keep top of mind in your pursuit of great relationships.

Chapter 4 • The Brainy Truth

Get in on the Ground Floor

When thinking shifts, change happens.

Thinking is the basis of everything. It is the foundation of who we are and what we do. Everything flows from our thinking. Consider this: Our thinking leads to our emotions. Our emotions direct and impact behaviors. Behaviors then lead to our outcomes and results.

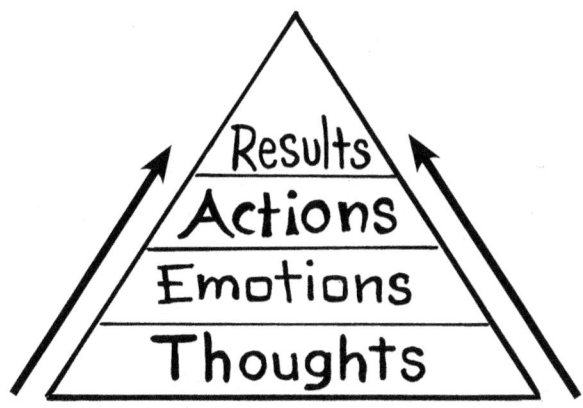

Understanding this sequencing is essential if you want to get to new and lasting results. This works for any kind of new result you want. I know it did for me, 50 pounds ago.

Yes, my 5'2" frame used to carry that additional weight, and it did for about 12 years. But one day I decided I wanted to do something about that number on the scale – that was after I was willing to *see, believe,* and *own* it. I was longing for a new result – a new me.

My past experience would've led me to start exercising more and eating less. (Both of those are behaviors). I didn't do that. Instead, I picked up a health book and started reading. Then another and another.

You know what was happening? My thinking was changing. I began learning. I became aware and started having aha moments. That was the trigger.

As my thinking shifted, I got head-smart about my body, food and exercise, and that compelled me to get on the move (figuratively and literally). This new thinking led me to new and improved emotions, behaviors and results.

Behavioral Changes Alone Don't Stick

Where is your natural starting point when you want to change your results? Think about your workplace – what gets the most focus when something or someone needs improvement? I doubt it's someone's thinking. But, you *can* start changing that.

Society is primarily setup to focus first on changing behaviors. The reason is simple: behaviors are visible and measurable.

Chapter 4 • The Brainy Truth

There is some truth and short-term gain in behavioral change, but you must know that it is typically short-lived.

Long-term change that sticks always involves new thinking. And tapping into thinking first is efficient and effective – really. It's just smart. Because this is how the brain works.

Reflection is a great way to inspire new thinking and new ideas. It allows you to see things you hadn't seen before and provides a chance of gaining *new* insight into a current problem, issue or dilemma. The questions below are great ways to get reflection powers revved-up.

Reflection Questions
• What ideas or thoughts have crossed your mind that you might have dismissed?
• What are some different ways you could tackle this situation?
• Can you see this problem from another angle?
• What other options come to mind for you?
• What would you really like to achieve here?
• If you could have anything in this area, what would it be?

Making changes for you and helping others create change is expanded greatly when you camp out on thinking. In boardrooms and at kitchen tables, this is frequently missed.

But the opportunity to turn that around is here, now. The Delightful Dozen questions and the Reflection questions are tools that keep you focused on supporting the other person's thinking. With that, you are able to shorten your conversations, carry fewer burdens about having all the answers for someone else, and help others discover their own new ideas.

Now that you see the value of having a thinking focus, let's further explore the brainy things that happen the moment new thinking is born.

An insight is the "Ka-POW" that happens in the brain when you've created new thinking. You may have called it a light bulb moment or an aha. It is seeing something like you haven't before.

Can you think of a time when you've had one of those moments? What do you recall about what triggered it? How did it feel? What were you motivated to do?

As I coach clients, my goal is always the same: help them create new thinking and insights. This is where the fun begins in this highly Collaborative and Connected process.

Chapter 4 • The Brainy Truth

Tap into the "Ka-POW"

Inspiring and helping others to have insights is priority #1 for the true Connector and for the leader who empowers.

Brains are insight machines; they just need a little jumpstarting. Insights are born in the brain. You can help someone have an insight, but you can't have one for another person. That's just how it works.

Oftentimes things go awry when you attempt to insert your ideas and great thinking into someone else's mind. Even if the other person accepts what you offer, that insight will always be yours. Bottom line: I must have my insight and you must have yours. There's no other way.

In my relationships and conversations, I want the very best possible result. Second-best is not worth going for. The very best is. So let's go for that and shake up how we do things. Let's learn more about creating insights.

Why are Insights so Special?

Because they propel people to take big, new action steps toward their goals.

Insights are just waiting to be born. Brains are unique powerhouses with intricate wiring, and no two are alike. It's key that you really grasp that.

My brain-wiring and yours do not have the same points of reference because my wiring has been created and established through my lifetime of learning and experiences. The same is true for you.

For example, if I asked 20 people to tell me the first word that comes to mind when I say the word, "game," I would get an array of answers. Try it. What comes to mind is directed by each individual's unique brain wiring. Insights are as unique and distinct as the individuals creating them.

What Does that Teach Us About Insights?

First, you cannot create an insight for someone else; it's impossible. Give up trying to do so, because it wastes time and leaves you with less than the best. Instead, support others having insights for themselves. Just like a doctor assists a mother who is having a baby, you can assist another person in creating an insight. It truly is a birthing process.

Second, insights reveal individual expression and creativity. As you help others create new thinking, you open the door for innovation. This can't be forced; it happens when it is allowed to emerge.

How is an Insight Triggered?

Look back at the Delightful Dozen questions and Reflection questions earlier in this chapter – these are insight instigators! Typically insights are gleaned when you receive new information or are asked a question that causes you to think about something in a new way. They can also come in the middle of the night when your brain is focused elsewhere but your subconscious mind is working on things.

As you reflect and consider something new, you are using brain power as it runs up and down existing brain pathways. An

The Art of Relationship-ing

insight occurs when existing wires come together to create a new connection. Think about it like a road that is intersected by another road, which then leads you to that third road. Roads 1 and 3 weren't connected, before. Now they are.

"What-if"-ing is another creative way to help others gain insight, while simultaneously Connecting and Collaborating. I was recently introduced to this approach by my colleague, Mindy Audlin. It helps expand thinking so the brain will be primed – and it's very easy to implement.

Simply add "what if," in front of the advice or opinion you're tempted to offer a colleague or friend who has a dilemma or issue to be solved. Giving someone an opportunity for insight is generous and productive – for both of you. It's far better than simple acceptance of and compliance with your ideas or suggestions. You give away the power and you facilitate collaboration.

Instead of This	Try This
Just call her and tell her what you think.	What if you called her and shared your opinion?
Don't hire an assistant to do that task.	What if you didn't hire an assistant for the work?
I would not do it like that.	What if you tried doing that a different way?

What Does an Insight Create?

Insights provide super-fuel for the brain. Natural, self-generated fuel is ready in an instant when someone has a moment of insight. Yep, gas is in the tank, and you're ready to get on the road. You are flooded with feelings that result in new clarity and awareness. You're ready to commit to action now.

What's really terrific is that when an insight is born, there's a physical charge in the brain. A "Ka-POW!" It's electric. I often hear my clients simply say, "Wow, *that's* it!" Or, "Gosh. I hadn't seen that until just now."

You begin envisioning what's possible, and you're ready to get onto the pathway to creating new emotions and behaviors which lead to new outcomes.

What's all the Buzz About Insights?

If you've ever had an insight, you know, because you've just created something with your own brain power. It's exhilarating, empowering and confidence-building.

And once someone has an insight, typically the person is self-motivated. The best part? It releases you from the burden of being the motivator. When someone has an insight, the person is now driven by a big spirit of "want to" around this new area of insight. When a person shifts from "have to" mode to "want to" mode, it's huge. Stop and think about how significant that is!

When you have an employee, team member, family member or friend who is operating out of "have to" *that* places a heavy burden of responsibility on you to ensure that the other person is giving enough and doing enough so that you're getting what you need and want. Do you see that?

Another disadvantage of operating in "have to" mode is that most people are compelled to give only the minimum required. Geesh – that doesn't give your business, your team, or any relationship, much of a chance for being great or achieving excellence!

"Want to" mode is clearly preferable at home and in workplace relationships.

As a recap, here's how you arrive at this great place – "want to" mode. Remember that Step #1 is done by you. The remaining steps are generated by the other person. Again, *your* action as the Connector is in Step #1 – that's it.

1. *You* help inspire someone to create new thinking.

2. This new thinking results in the person having an insight.

3. The person with the insight experiences new awareness.

4. The person with the insight feels new motivation.

5. The person with the insight shifts into "want to" mode.

Notice that new thinking is what started this whole process. That's why you want to become expert at inspiring it in others. You're beginning to see how making all of this happen in your conversations *is* possible. It all starts with your helping others create new thinking.

Now, let's expand your Brainy Truths a little further. Read on to learn and become aware of the brain's top three preferences. These will help you continue to navigate conversations smartly and efficiently, while Connecting and relationship-ing in a whole new way.

Brainflash:
"Smart Relationship-ers Maneuver Finicky Brains"

Every brain has preferences. I have highlighted the top three brain preferences as 'Headlines' in this section of the book. Knowing and applying them will enable you to Connect with others more quickly, with more meaning, and have productive conversations with greater ease.

When you are mindful of these three preferences, others' brains will give you the green light and will welcome your conversation and presence. But, if you disregard these preferences, you risk their brains putting on the brakes because you could be seen as a red light.

In order to create green light conversations and Connections, begin embracing these headlines today!

Headline #1 – My brain likes my ideas best.

This is true for your clients, colleagues, friends and family members. Let this sink in.

Write the headline on a note card and place it somewhere that you'll glance at often. Keep this in mind, as this truth is a mental shift of trust, belief and generosity.

This headline gives you another reason why your best approach is to help others create their own new ideas and innovative thinking. Brains will never like or be inspired by your advice or ideas like they will be by their own.

Great, meaningful Connection happens when you create the physical and mental space for others to bring their brain power and their unique brain-mapping to the conversation. You either create space for others to do that, or you don't.

Here are some ways of creating "safe" brain space for others. These tips put brains at ease so you have a great chance of being well received.

- Ask questions that cause others to reflect on their own thinking (around their idea, dilemma or situation). Hopefully these questions lead someone to have a moment of insight. Refer back to the Reflection questions earlier in this chapter.

- "Check" your title and your status at the door. This puts the other person's brain at ease and establishes a spirit of equality between you.

- Explain your agenda, if you have one. Uncertainty is scary for the brain. Just like a scared child wants to run away and hide, the scared brain does the same thing. Creating certainty minimizes or diffuses that.

- Share control. People feel empowered when they get to exert control over decisions that impact them. Consider how you can make this happen. The brain likes choice. When we have choices, we get to use our brains to make decisions. That may sound simple, but it's true. And we get this wrong – a lot.

- Be relatable. Establishing this upfront puts you in the friend category (as opposed to foe). When you take the initiative on this, you'll speed up safety for the other person's brain. In short, my brain says, "If I can relate to you, I'm willing to let down my guard and open up a bit. I begin to trust you because I feel known by you." Can you see it?

Chapter 4 • The Brainy Truth

- Be fair. If something doesn't seem fair to someone, brains shout out, "No fair." Then they shut down. When you make a conversation or decision fair, even if it's a tough one, you've considered the other person. Having others perceive you as fair is huge. Fair people are considerate, transparent, honest and practical – all at once. They can go far with others quickly because of who they've established themselves to be. Brains open up to those fair souls in our lives. Be one.

Each of these tips is dependent on you. Each one must be pursued with authenticity. Fakeness and manipulation around any one of these will put you on a relationship crash course. Please don't do that. Always choose the high road.

Headline #2 – Asking permission opens doors.

Brains like being asked something rather than being told something.

As a coach, this is a principle I learned early on. It is incredibly effective. Here are some examples of using permission:

- May I ask you a question about ____ ? (perhaps it's something the person mentioned to you earlier in the conversation that you *really* heard because of your Dynamic Duo Listening)

- Would you like to brainstorm some ideas about how we could work together on that problem?

- Can I share an experience I recently had that relates to your issue?

- Could I give you my two cents on your dilemma?

- May I give you a suggestion on how we can make the situation better?

Here's the kicker: when you ask permission, you have to be ready to receive an answer – yes or no. In my experience, when I ask permission, I hear "yes" about 99% of the time. But when I hear "no" I honor it and move on, acceptingly.

Permission is also perceived as transparency – which feels safe to the brain. When the brain is safe, connection and collaboration are possible, and that's the goal in *The Art of Relationship-ing*.

The other wonderful thing that permission can do is save you both time and energy. Take this question as an example. "Would you like my help in providing names of resources for that project?"

If you didn't ask that question, but instead just worked on providing that list, you could be wasting time. By asking, you might've learned that resources had already been selected, and the current need is elsewhere.

Finally, permission allows you to gain the insider view of things, because it's common that when you ask and then listen, you'll learn (and not assume). Recall what you learned about Dynamic Duo Listening earlier in this chapter.

Headline #3 – Mind your own brain.

Embracing this truth will cause you to speak less, listen differently, and engage more.

All of our Brainy Truths build upon each other. This one really drives it home: I like my brain, and I like to use my brain. The same is true for you and others. When you are constantly trying to direct someone else's thoughts, it creates congestion and frustration for that person. At some point, that person's brain will shut off access to you. And, you don't want that.

Instead, embrace that brains are created to process. It feels good; everyone wants to contribute. Create the space for that to happen for others by using the Delightful Dozen questions, Reflection questions and the "What-if"-ing approach discussed earlier in this chapter.

By knowing the brain's top three preferences, you'll tap into all of the goodies that Brainy Truths have to offer. Green light conversations will be your modus operandi.

In addition to these three brain preferences, you've learned these Brainy Truths:

- You've caught a new view of Brain Science.

- You've seen what's in it for you.

- You've learned how thinking is where change begins.

- You've gained new tools to help you inspire new thinking in others.

- You've seen how insights are created.

- You've learned about the bounty that comes after insight.

In the final section of this chapter, you'll focus on making new commitments around your new Brainy Truths.

Make a Difference by Making a Change

Now that you have all this new Brain Science knowledge, what will you do next?

Chapter 4 • The Brainy Truth

It's time to bridge the gap between your new thoughts and your commitment – it's time to take action. This is your chance to stop being a conversation controller and start being a Connection innovator.

Is there a great divide between who you are right now and the kind of Connector you would like to be? If so, that gap represents what's between you and your having great relationships. The first step of closing the gap begins with casting a vision and making a commitment.

So, put your pen to paper – create a relationship manifesto for yourself. Answer these questions by creating commitment statements:

- Who do you want to *be* in your relationships?

- How do you envision your new relationship mission kicking off?

- What could be possible if you made relationships #1 on your priority list?

- What do you need to *be* or do to sync your talk with your walk?

- Who will you begin relationship-ing with differently?

- What will you start doing today to implement change?

How, where and with whom you apply your new Brainy Truths will be a creative excursion. Anything involving people is dynamic and fluid – not prescriptive. Take your new smarts, make them yours, and adventure into your relationships with your new truths and tools. Using these tools will enable you to see what makes a difference in your relationships.

Now that you have the new Brainy Truths to become a great Connector, you're ready for the next chapter, Gender Smarter. There, you'll learn how to have greater synergy and Collaboration between the sexes.

Chapter 4 • The Brainy Truth

Chapter 5

Gender Smarter

"It's a very special human quality that allows us to step outside of ourselves and try to understand another person from within."

– Leo Buscaglia

The Art of Relationship-ing

Men and women are *designed* very differently – and that's for a purpose. Seeing the strengths in both genders, points the way to illumination, understanding and appreciation. This new awareness leads to simpler ways of creating collaboration instead of confusion and adds a whole new dimension to your relationship equation.

Understanding helps avoid misunderstanding. And boy, do we want to avoid it. Misunderstanding is the tipping point for irritation, frustration, lack of focus and wasted time – all of which make relationships harder than necessary. So let's change that.

Picture this: a whisk and a hammer. These are two tools that most of us have and use. They are functional and useful. Why? Because we understand their purpose and design. If we didn't, we would be frustrated, needlessly.

For example, let's say I am in the kitchen. I crack five eggs in a bowl and want to beat them for an omelette.

I have two tools available to use for this task: the whisk and the hammer.

I choose to use the hammer, so I place its handle in the bowl of eggs and stir. It may be clunky, but I get the eggs beaten enough for my omelette. So I was able to get the result I wanted. It wasn't pretty, nor was it easy, but I was successful.

Let's shift the setup a bit.

Now I want to make a meringue topping for a coconut cream pie. I place five egg whites in the bowl and need to beat them to stiff peaks. Again, I have two tools available (whisk and hammer), and I choose the hammer. Just as before, I use the handle end of the hammer and begin beating the egg whites. Will I ever get to stiff peaks? Even with lots of commitment, effort, time and focus?

No. It just won't happen.

I chose a tool that wasn't designed or purposed for this job. I can try and try, but I will not get to the result I want. My lack of understanding about the tool caused me to waste time, become

The Art of Relationship-ing

frustrated and fall short of my goal. Knowing the purpose of the tool up front would've made all the difference.

The same is true with your understanding of men and women. As you know and understand their purposes, you have greater awareness of how to work smartly with them.

You may say that you know how different the genders are, but I have found that people don't *live* like they know it. As a result, relationships are less fulfilling and Collaborative than they could be. I want you to have more in your relationships – that begins by becoming Gender Smarter!

Back to that egg white example. Since I understand the purpose of a hammer, I would never, ever expect it to produce stiffly beaten egg whites.

I also wouldn't waste time or energy lamenting the fact that the hammer isn't more like the whisk. Nor would I begin making sweeping statements about the whisk being the superior tool. All of this would be ridiculous! I mean who would ever consider all of that? But, we would and we do when it comes to our views about men and women. My goal is to stop this craziness.

Repeat this: He ≠ She ≠ He.

This will always be true. And there's goodness and bounty in this truth.

When we're stuck in the land of misunderstanding, we can't see the beautiful rainbow overhead. Nor can we see the pot of gold at the end of it.

So again, He ≠ She ≠ He.

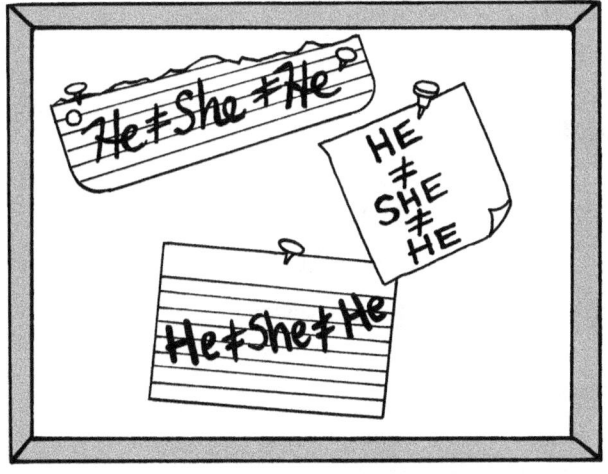

An apple is not an orange (although they are both fruit). A whisk is not a hammer (although both are tools). A 3-iron is not a pitching wedge (although both are golf clubs).

Once more, He ≠ She ≠ He.

Benefits to Becoming Gender Smarter

The benefits that you get by being Gender Smarter are out of this world! They will enable you to R-E-A-C-H new heights in your relationships:

- **R** enewed focus
- **E** mpowerment
- **A** wareness
- **C** larity
- **H** ealing

Renewed Focus

With new focus, you see, believe and tap into the distinctive strengths of others. You are on a completely new pathway to collaboration, and it's an expressway.

Empowerment

Learning what you and others are best designed to do is empowering and freeing. It's liberating, too. Gender Smarts put new wind in your sails. They allow you to go further with more ease and synchronicity in your relationships.

Awareness

Having aha and light bulb moments are guaranteed. Get ready to be saying and thinking, "Oh, wow – that never made sense until *now*!" Here, you will *get it* and set aside irritation and frustration and move forward with new insights on how you can begin Collaborating smartly – together.

Clarity

Your mind will be clearer as you begin seeing how easily you can reduce the static in your relationships. You will see where you need and want to make changes in you, so that you'll reap the benefits of these changes in your relationships. That will give you more harmony and productivity in achieving the results you want. With clarity, you'll say, "Okay. *Now* I see what's going on here." Then you're ready to take action.

Healing

As you begin living the truth of He ≠ She ≠ He, your feelings, of hurt and disrespect will lessen. Some of them may completely vanish. It's incredible. You're likely to realize that your hurt or frustration happened more because of your misunderstanding than someone else's bad behavior.

As I speak to groups, this area of Gender Smarts gets a lot of attention and feedback – many laughs, too. I commonly hear, "*That's* what was driving his/her action?" And, "All along, I thought it was _____" (fill in the blank). For example, have you ever wondered how a man can walk out of his bedroom and step right over a pair of dirty socks and keep going without picking them up? You might've thought he was being disrespectful or careless. But, that's not the case. You'll understand that better when you read about He-focus in the next section.

Becoming Gender Smarter was a significant tipping point for me. It impacted all of my relationships – personally and professionally. I expected and wanted to improve my relationships with men, and I did. Plus there was a side benefit that I didn't expect – I learned more about my same sex which surprisingly deepened and expanded those relationships.

So, as you explore the Gender Smarts principles, cast your net really wide – and your mind, as well. You'll be surprised where it gets you. First up, I'll tell you about the surprising distinctions around focus and how they differ for men and women. This will kick-start your journey to becoming Gender Smarter.

Part I:
He-focus and She-focus

Men and women have a completely different relationship to "focus." Both have strengths; they're just different. One is not better than the other. There's no benefit to one-upping here.

Seeing a man's and a woman's strengths will equip you with new smarts on working with and alongside each gender. It's here that you will truly understand the different views. You will also begin seeing how you can pair the two together for maximum benefit.

He-focus

Simply defined: one thing at a time

The dictionary.com definition of "focus" is quite fitting for He-focus: "central point of attraction, attention or activity." Webster.com describes it as a "point of concentration."

Focus, in this context, means honing in on one thing and holding it front and center. It makes me think of a movie I saw where a fighter pilot locked his radar onto the enemy, and then launched his missiles. The "beep-beep-beep" sound began from the moment of the lock-in until the missile hit the target.

As men focus, they lock in on one thing, one problem, one person. They focus one-at-a-time. Yes, they can manage and handle many things, one-at-a-time. And guess what? That's how *both* male and female brains process things – one-at-a-time.

Zoom lens focus

In simple terms, it is pointed and direct. A man has a mission in mind of what he's setting out to do, and that mission holds his focus. It can relate to anything from a project at work to watching a football game, to walking from his bedroom to the front door.

Whatever the focus is, that's where his attention is.

Think of a zoom lens on a camera. He-focus zooms in on one object, person or situation, and everything else is out of frame. Things in his periphery are not being ignored; they just don't have his attention or his awareness. This is how a man can step over a pair of socks on the floor and keep moving – it's possible he didn't even notice them.

He is doing what comes naturally

This kind of power focus is primarily masculine. Men, who average 16-times the testosterone levels of women, are fueled by hormones to hunt an object or person, and therefore, they He-focus with relative ease. It is the default for them.

Women can access this level of focus, but it is not their default. Just as a man's brain physiology and hormones work to support He-focus, a woman's works to naturally support She-focus. As you will see later, the two are quite different.

Getting the job done

He-focus enables great productivity and results, with relatively few internal distractions. Accomplishment and completion are the name of the game.

Even though a man may have multiple priorities at one time, when his He-focus is activated, the one priority he has chosen is his only aim. And while his focus is here, the other priorities are set aside, as it's not yet their turn.

For men, those other priorities nicely and quietly sit on the sidelines. Lucky men! For women, competing priorities may sit on the sidelines, but they are seldom quiet.

Beware of perception

He-focus is a super power that comes with possible side effects. If I could bottle it up, I would attach this warning label:

CAUTION:

**May cause confusion in others –
use special care when administered near women.**

**Efficacy is further expanded
when taken around extreme stress or importance.**

Consider the view of an outsider – man or woman – who is observing a man with his He-focus turned "on." It will appear that he has tunnel-vision. He may also be perceived as rude, selfish, disconnected, oblivious and careless. It's a terrible list, I know.

For the He-focuser, these possible misperceptions seem ridiculous and completely off-base. Maybe so. But to the one who is misunderstanding you, these perceptions are reality.

Take precautionary steps

Consider taking these steps before you activate your He-focus power:

- Communicate to those around you – coworkers, family members, colleagues and friends – what it is that you're about to do. Tell them what to expect. Inform them that you're about to invoke your He-focus zoom-lens and will be fully consumed by _____ (fill in the blank). Also provide your time frame if possible.

- Ask for what you need. Let those people impacted by your He-focus know what you need in order to achieve your goal (i.e. no interruptions, quiet, etc.).

- Offer to provide something in return. Here's an example: "I am available to help you anytime today with our team's monthly sales analysis; however, tomorrow I'm fully committed to the Anderson proposal." Do you see how this tip can be like money in the bank? First, it provides for another's need. Then, in turn, it prevents interruptions and gives you the time you need to be in your He-focus zone. It also lessens the chance of your becoming frustrated by anyone or anything that distracts you. Ah, this is preventive maintenance – very smart.

She-focus

Simply defined: many things at once

It's not He-focus at all. She-focus begins with an intention to focus on something – on one thing. Women like and desire focus just as men do, but it just doesn't look the same for women.

Imagine focus with a split-personality. No, actually multiple personalities. That gets close to what She-focus is. It is focus that is given to a multitude of people, places and priorities.

As women exist, they live in She-focus. It's not a choice or a decision. It's their default. That is likely an unpopular statement, but it's true. And in truth, women have the power to tackle anything. Let's go a little deeper with this.

Wide-angle lens focus

With She-focus, a woman has a mission in mind, and she gets going on it. From preparing a meeting agenda to having a phone conversation, to walking from one room in the house to the next, She-focus is just waiting to be activated.

As a woman sets out on her mission, she naturally has one lens to use, the wide-angle lens. No zoom lens is in her *default* design. So with the wide-angle lens, she has one thing as the intended focus, with lots and lots of space for other things in her frame.

A woman's focus is inclusive. As this is true, lots of things call for and get her attention at once. Yes, a variety of individual things are getting done, one-at-a-time.

A common misperception is that women are masters of multitasking. The illusionary definition for that is "getting many things accomplished at the same time." It just isn't possible or true. Womens' brains do not work that way; mens' brains don't either. Think about this: if you're listening to a conference call while writing an email, only one thing is in the foreground, and getting your primary attention. Don't be fooled into believing otherwise. It's just not how the brain works.

She is doing what comes naturally

With its wide-angle lens, She-focus provides an incredible view of all the things going on around the primary task at hand. Women's hormones, which prompt nurturing and caretaking, fuel the multifaceted nature of She-focus. Women's brain physiology wires them to be like human satellite dishes – picking up, processing and transmitting all of the varied emotional and physical signals that come within its inclusive range.

I recently learned that women's peripheral vision is, on average, greater than men's. Geesh! Hormones, brain physiology and even physical vision explain how women self-fuel this powerful She-focus.

Taking it ALL in

She-focus takes in an almost inexplicable amount of data, happenings and occurrences. A woman's receptors are continually absorbing the many things around her mission. The "many things" that come into her frame become mini-priorities.

Her mission was the initial plan and priority, but once she embarks onto the playing field where the mission is, it's as if all at once, all of the things that were on the sidelines suddenly rush onto the field – and they are all calling out for attention.

Silent but loudly perceived are the shouts, "Hey! Over here! What about me? Look at this! Don't forget that! Oh, I only need a minute." The natural She-focuser tends to each of the mini-priorities with swiftness; she's on the move, on the go, getting it all done.

Women see and perceive with such a broad view. It's exhilarating and bustling. She-focus misses very little in her surroundings.

Beware of perception

She-focus is indeed a super power that both provides a lot and costs a lot.

In all of the moving and shaking that goes along with She-focus, there are many distractions. They become focus stealers – thieves! They shout for her attention and get it. Then there's a need for even more energy and focus to get back to the initial priority or mission. You know – the REAL one.

I recently experienced this. I was working in my home office and was initially tapped into He-focus (yes, it is possible for one gender to take on tendencies of the other). That He-focus lasted until I needed to refill my glass of water. So, I picked it up and walked to the kitchen.

Along the way, I passed by the bathroom and turned off the light. Then I walked down the hall and saw a fur ball (thanks to my dog, Riley), so I picked it up. Once I got to the kitchen, I tossed the fur ball into the trash and noticed that it was getting full. Might as well take it out, so I did.

Once outside, I checked the mail, walked back into the house and set the mail down on the table. I then thought, "Okay. Better get back to work!" I walked back to my office, sat down, and started working. Then, I reached for my glass of water. What glass of water? The one that wasn't there. Darn – that was my mission, and the distracters (aka mini-priorities) diverted my mission. I never did fill up my water glass. This is an example of what happens in She-focus every day.

What did all of this cost me, and what does it cost women who are in She-focus mode? Time and energy. Unfortunately, women often forego their intended priorities and the desired outcomes. My glass of water is a simple metaphor for a greater truth: allowing distractions to trump your mission leaves you empty-handed or with delayed achievement.

Women then get overwhelmed about their lack of completion or accomplishment. And, that feeling is costly. It further slows down the ability to focus and accomplish. Ugh!

Chapter 5 • Gender Smarter

Here are the perceptions that others may have about the She-focuser. She seems:

- Disorganized
- Scattered
- Uncommitted
- Slow
- Overly-accommodating

Thinking back to my water glass example, I can see how someone could have perceived each of these things about me. I know these qualities don't describe me. I was simply on the move and getting things done. Just different things than I had initially planned. But hey, they needed to get done at some point – so why not right then?

The perceptions others have are important to know because they impact Collaboration and effectiveness. We can't ignore perception if we desire great relationships.

So let's get ahead of it.

A remedy for all those distractions

Here are some practical ways women can manage their lifelong, instinctive tendency of She-focus:

1. *Clear your space physically and mentally.* What could you do before you start on your task that would help clear your mind and your physical area so you had fewer distractions?

2. *Speak out your mission (yes, aloud).* Whether it's big or small, verbally say what it is you are setting out to do. This helps you to hear it, focus on it, and remember it. It may sound funny, but who cares. It will help you stay committed to achieving your mission.

3. *Say "no" to the sideline distractions.* When the mini-priorities start surfacing and begin threatening your mission, think or say, "not now." Add them to a list of things to consider later.

4. *Ask for help and receive it.* The She-focuser can feel like she's at the bottom of an ever-growing mountain of priorities. To scale any mountain, you need equipment, resources and tools. You cannot do all of it by yourself. Be willing to ask for help from people. After all, relationships are about giving – *and receiving.*

Once you ask for help, express your need clearly along with any details that are essential. Remember that no one will complete the task exactly as you would have done it – so don't expect that. What's key is that the task is being accomplished, or at least started, with someone else's time, energy and effort – not yours. Be a gracious receiver.

Blending He-focus and She-focus

A terrific combination is possible when you combine the strengths of He-focus and She-focus.

The two complement each other nicely and powerfully. What one lacks, the other makes possible. Are you beginning to see how He-focus and She-focus Collaboration can expand what you are able to achieve?

Consider how much more effective a board meeting could be if you had the blended powers of He-focus and She-focus teamed together and working to achieve your desired outcome. Or, how about leading a training class or planning a family reunion? Yes, more is possible when you mindfully pair He-focus and She-focus.

How could these new Gender Smarts make a difference for you – at work and at home?

Start planning for that now. Make a list of three actions you will take to implement what you've already learned in this chapter.

Now that you have a greater understanding of He-focus and She-focus, you are equipped to begin Collaborating smartly, efficiently and with more meaning – because you now *get* focus and know how to work with it.

Part II:
Meet Mr. Provider and Ms. Connector

Knowing both gender's primary drivers enables you to see how each naturally wants and tries to contribute in relationships. In this section, you will learn how you can best give and receive – to and from both genders.

Men are primarily designed to *Provide* just as women are designed and purposed to *Connect*. Knowing this helps you to understand the driver that is behind each gender's actions.

Too many times we evaluate and judge actions or words based on our perception of where the person is "coming from." Those perceptions are often misperceptions, and they wreak unnecessary havoc in our relationships. Let's change this by illuminating reality.

Men Are Driven to Provide

A man is at his very best when he is Providing. This desire is often subconscious, but it's always present.

The Provider is opportunistic. He is "on," ready, willing and able to Provide at a moment's notice. He sees, listens, and observes through the spirit of a Provider.

He feels an urge and often a responsibility to contribute answers and solutions with words and actions.

Ladies, have you ever been discussing something with a man and experienced him jumping into the conversation with his turbo-powered ideas that were likely very different from your ideas?

From his perspective, whether done well or not, he was attempting to Provide for you. He had an idea, opinion or insight that he believed would contribute to your getting to your best outcome. That's what was going on! He wasn't trying to be assuming, domineering or impatient. The driver beneath his action or response was to provide – for you! Really, it's that simple.

Men, this quality in you is unique and special. It is generous. You want to be sure to use it mindfully, so it will not be misunderstood. Unfortunately, it often is, especially by women who haven't learned this Gender Smart truth about you.

Be on the lookout for the Provider in yourself – listen to your words, look at your actions, and notice your thinking. It's everywhere; do you see it?

Next, realize that a Provider unleashed can be perceived as a bully; and no one likes a bully. I want you to be both liked and well-received by others. So this will require some attention by you. It will pay off and empower you to be a new kind of Collaborator.

Quick tips to maximize *Provider* power:

- Understand what someone needs or wants before you dive into Provider mode. Gaining understanding of this first will enable you to be an A+ Provider. Ask before you advise or fix. It will save you from your best intentions being tossed into the trash can.

- Peek back into the Brainy Truth section of this book for smart ways to open up conversations and kick-start Collaboration. Using those tools will equip you to smartly place your Provider power in the place that will support, and not overrun, others. This is the mark of a smart and collaborative Provider.

Women Are Designed to Connect

Women are Connection machines! They are "on the ready" to seek and establish Connection when they feel safe and valued. Without safety and value, women will hold back their Connection tendencies. We don't want this, because women are their very best when they are living into and through their Connection greatness.

Men, can you relate to this? It is a conversation you've had with a woman. Well, actually, in this conversation you were listening to her more than anything. She was sharing detail after detail about something that happened or something she did. It probably felt like you were listening to a baseball announcer giving play-by-play details. While this may frustrate you, this is how she Connects.

It's possible that, as a man, you were wondering, "What's the point?" Or, "Is all of this detail going to matter?" Or, "Can you give me the bottom line?" As the Provider, you were considering how much of this you needed to know in order to help her with something that she *surely* needed help with, right?

Thinking back to that conversation, did it seem to end with no climax? Maybe it just ended. Do you know why? Because it wasn't about a problem or a need. To the Connector, it was all about sharing.

Her silent voice says this – when I feel safe and valued by you (man or woman), I share my experiences in detail. Then you will know me and understand me. As you do, you'll *get me,* and voila, we'll have a connection. That connection adds to my value of you and our relationship. I want to give my best to those with whom I share these kinds of relationships.

Yes, that's how the puzzle comes together. Do you see it now?

If the Connector's sharing process continually gets halted by the listener, the Connector will begin to shut down. So will the quality of the relationship.

Women, your ability to Connect with others is superb and gives spice to life. I want you to use it and have access to all its beauty, like an artist uses a wide array of colors. Here's what you can do to help make this happen, so it honors you and creates an opportunity for great connection to happen for you.

Quick tips to maximize *Connector* power:

- Get clear up front on what you need and want to have for a good connection.

- Ask for or schedule the amount of time and attention you'll need. (Don't leave it to happenstance).

- Begin the conversation with your main point. (Or maybe your point is that there is no point and you simply need to share a story or experience).

- Be fully "you," and help others learn how to receive you as Ms. Connector (all of these points make that happen). Be patient and persistent as this is a new way of introducing Mr. Provider and Ms. Connector.

Mr. Provider + Ms. Connector = Destiny

This world is inhabited by men and women, and working together is our destiny and reality. Our paths will constantly be crossing.

Becoming Gender Smarter enables you to better Collaborate in your relationships and makes for a smoother and easier journey. At the same time, the results you will achieve together, through Collaboration, are more meaningful.

Your secret power is your knowledge of each gender's design and purpose. You are now smarter, wiser, and more efficient in how you work with men and women. New possibilities are at your fingertips now that you've met and understood Mr. Provider and Ms. Connector. The opposite sex is no longer a mystery. You're beginning to truly comprehend male and female drivers.

Next up is Part III – it sheds new light on how each gender communicates and what that *looks* and *sounds* like.

Part III:
Men of Actions and Women of Words

Show me. Tell me. Both are ways of communicating that we use daily. Taking action reveals and expresses by producing an *outward result*. Whereas giving words shares and offers intention or commitment by creating a *verbal connection*.

People crave both: seeing actions and hearing words.

The Art of Relationship-ing

Think of your performance at work. I recall a manager who once told me that his feedback approach was "no news is good news." If he thought I was doing a great job, he would indicate that to me by being silent. But, if he had a problem with something, he said he would be sure to let me know. The other way he said he would give positive feedback would be by rewarding me with a commensurate annual pay increase.

I loathed his feedback system. It did not work for me. I needed and wanted to be both shown and told how I was doing.

I wish I had known then what I know now; I could've used my Brainy Truths and Gender Smarts to Connect and Collaborate with my manager and strike a deal that worked for both of us. I would've expressed my need (for verbal feedback) succinctly – then explained to him how he could Provide for that need (through both words and actions). Finally, I would've shared what that style of feedback would enable in me (greater confidence and empowerment).

Let's learn from my boss what not to do. Simply stated – a better way to create and maintain great relationships is by balancing the use of actions and words.

Men tend to speak more through actions, whereas women tend to speak through words. Again, even these gender tendencies and defaults are based on differing brain physiology and hormones. Interesting how that truth shows up again.

Men prefer to *show* what they think or feel by *doing* something. In taking action, they express themselves and show others what they are committed to and what they value – by doing something. For men, commitment comes before action.

Women like to *express* what they think and feel by *telling* you. In sharing words, they communicate their emotions, feelings, instincts, perspectives and insights.

Words give depth and heart. Through words, women are creating Connections which you read about earlier. For women, words can give the full story and are filled with fact, intention, belief and passion. In giving words, she gives her truth – her best. Words become her best expression of self.

Scene One: Man-brain and Woman-brain

Mens' actions are fueled by logic, and women's words are fueled by emotion. Our different brains explain why.

While in a conversation, men have less connection or access to their feelings than women. Their default question isn't, "How did that make me *feel*," but instead, "What do I want to do about this?" In this instance, men primarily tap into left (logical) brain thinking.

Men don't place high value or importance on feelings, because they are not key drivers. Men are constantly doing a consistency check between what's going on right in front of them and how that compares to their values and beliefs. If his consistency check causes a warning light to come on, he will take action.

This looks different for women. Womens' right (emotional) brains and left (logical) brains have many connectors. This enables women to have a conversation, feel an emotion and in an instant, gain access to many words to describe their feelings.

Men have fewer of those left-brain to right-brain connectors. Neither sex is better or worse off because of this. But it does shed light on gender differences.

Scene Two: Then There Was a Spat

Let's look at one example. A man and woman are having an argument. In the heat of the moment, a woman is really in touch with how she's feeling. She's accessing her many high-powered left-brain to right-brain connectors and attaching her feelings to words. And whoosh! She has an avalanche of words that she begins giving the man. For him, this can seem like one of those magic shows where all of these things are happening and appearing, but it's not clear what's going on. It's mind-boggling!

And the man is speechless; he's not sure what he's even feeling in this millisecond. And he certainly has not accessed any words quite yet to describe it. He's likely quiet because he honestly has nothing to say. Or, not yet.

Women are standing "on the ready," with their words and emotions and are often confused by men's silence. That confusion quickly tips to frustration and misunderstanding – for both women and men. Why? Because without Gender Smarts, they don't *get* the other person. They haven't begun *living* the truth that He ≠ She ≠ He.

You are now becoming being Gender Smarter. You are understanding and seeing what is going on for each gender. In this scenario, nothing is wrong in either gender's response. The only thing that is wrong is how we often misunderstand one another. So let's right this wrong.

Scene Three: They Became Gender Smarter

To better Collaborate with men…

1. Learn to *hear* what a man's *actions* are saying. Listen newly and freshly.

2. Choose to value a man's actions, because they are expressing his commitment and truth. His best. This is also another way he taps into his key driver as Mr. Provider.

3. Make space for a "time out" when a conversation gets heated (this is good for both genders). Whoever asks for the "time out" holds the responsibility for getting everyone back together later to resolve things.

4. Remember that less is often more – with words. Consider how you can talk less and say more in your conversations.

To better Collaborate with women…

1. Learn to *hear* what matters most through the bounty of women's *words*. Refer back to Dynamic Duo Listening in the Brainy Truth chapter.

2. Choose to value her expression through words as it is how she gives the best of herself and taps into her key driver as Ms. Connector.

3. Call for a "time-out" when a conversation gets heated (this is good for both genders). Whoever asks for the "time out" holds the responsibility for getting everyone back together later to resolve things.

4. Remember that words are important to women; stretch yourself to achieve a good balance between doing and speaking in your relationships.

In the Trust chapter, you learned about apologies – what they are, what they do, and how they can become restoring agents. Next, you'll learn what goes on behind the scenes when those two simple words – I'm sorry – are felt, contemplated, and expressed. Knowing this will help you immediately.

Part IV:
The Deal with "I'm Sorry"

Men and women relate to the phrase, "I'm sorry" quite differently. That is an understatement. They relate to it completely differently.

Real relationships require frequent reconciliation. Understanding how each gender expresses sorrow will help clear the air and keep your relationships moving forward. In addition, gaining new awareness about each genders' apology preferences will stretch you to consider *giving* apologies in a new way.

As I became Gender Smarter about "I'm sorry," I began understanding what was going on behind the scenes. It made a tremendous difference for me and my relationships.

Women with the "I'm Sorry" That Really Isn't

Women have two uses for "I'm sorry." The first is light and casual and is frequently used. Start listening to women in casual conversation. You'll hear them (or yourself) use it more times than you can imagine. The use of "I'm sorry" is said in instances like these:

- when the checker at the grocery store drops your bag of apples

- when the waiter reaches across your table and spills a glass of water

- when you're talking to someone on a cell phone and there's a poor connection

What do you notice about these instances?

"I'm sorry" is said by the person who *didn't* cause the problem. Fascinating, isn't it? Most importantly, *there is no harm* that is done in these situations – no one was hurt. Here, "I'm sorry" doesn't express true sorrow. It simply means, "Oh, too bad that happened." There is no personal ownership to "I'm sorry" in this context.

Men and Women with the *Real* and *Authentic* "I'm Sorry"

The second way women use, "I'm sorry" is to take ownership for a hurt they caused another person. This is the one and only way men use "I'm sorry." So the use is the same. But, each gender's relationship to it and the depth of it is different – this is where the confusion and frustration exists.

Women express this authentic "I'm sorry" *in words* to communicate regret and begin the mending process. It means, "I was wrong in saying/doing that," or, "I wish I hadn't said/done that," or, "I am sorry I hurt you." They want your forgiveness so you can make up, restore your connection and move forward.

It is a verbal pursuit for reconnection. *Saying,* "I'm sorry" is easier for women than men because of womens' natural tendency to express with words. Continue on and you'll understand why.

Men view, "I'm sorry" as something heavy and deep. It's intense. For men, expressing, "I'm sorry" in words is difficult. It's like a proclamation of failure over the loud speaker. Defeat and disappointment are their primary feelings at that moment.

When I learned this, I was blown away.

Wow. "I'm sorry" is bigger to men than it is to women. This explained why men deliver, "I'm sorry" differently. As my Gender Smarts continued to build, I began *getting* men and seeing them in a whole new light in this area.

From what you learned earlier in this chapter, you won't be surprised to know that men prefer to express "I'm sorry" *through their actions*. When his actions say "I'm sorry," it's just as genuine as it would be with words – actually even more so. So that's what's going on with "I'm sorry."

Learning and embracing how each gender wants to receive and give "I'm sorry" is a great starting point. Read further to get really clear on how to do this.

Apology Likes and Needs

Recall from the Trust chapter that hurt people need to be healed, and it's healing that enables your relationships to be restored. Now, blend that truth with your new awareness of each gender's strengths, preferences, and defaults. Through your Gender Smarts, you now have heightened awareness of how to smartly, sincerely and compassionately restore damage in your relationships.

And, you have the power to be a master healer with your apologies. It requires your willingness, as this is a *generous shift* in how you relationship with others: *providing healing for them based on their preferences and needs.* Are you up for making this shift?

If so, healing the other person will become your first priority – because you know that the quality of your relationship depends upon it. As you adopt a new view of apologies and become the master healer, you will *sincerely* believe this:

> **I want your hurt to go away**
> *even when* **I don't understand the hurt or agree with it.**

As you do this with compassion, *you* will change – and *your relationships* will, too.

Read below for each gender's apology likes and needs. With this knowledge, you will be a big winner in healing others, and you'll get your relationships back on track with greater ease.

You should know this about women and "I'm sorry." Women...

- prefer to *speak* the words "I'm sorry" to another

- prefer to *hear* the words "I'm sorry" audibly when they've been hurt, offended or wronged

- need to *hear* specifically what you're sorry for and need to hear it like this: "I am sorry that I _____"

- need to *see* and *hear* your sincerity in "I'm sorry." You have to say it like you mean it; otherwise, you'll make it worse

You should know this about men and "I'm sorry." Men...

- prefer to *express* "I'm sorry" through their *actions* and need those actions to be received and understood as an apology

- are willing to *receive* an apology in either actions or words, so long as both are caring and sincere

- need to be able to move on after apologies are given without always having to hash it out in words

Apology with a New View – for Men *and* Women

When you're on the journey to *The Art of Relationship-ing*, you see relationships through a new lens. And, how you work through apologies will look different.

> Remember: A truly restoring apology is sincere and generous. It focuses on healing the person who is hurting, even when:
>
> - you didn't intend it
> - you don't understand it
> - it doesn't make sense

Here, you are sorry for the injury and take ownership for causing it.

The "sorry" is more about the hurt to the other person than the action that caused it. An apology given like this – whether in *words* or *actions* – is generous. It is off-the-charts caring and distinctly different from what our self-focused world promotes. This new apology view requires a *significant shift,* I know. You'll find that the results are well worth it – the quality of your relationships will prove it.

Part V:
Commit to a BIG Give

A big give is when you choose to give to someone in a way that is meaningful to that person even though it isn't natural or a default for you. This is extremely generous, considerate and caring. With your Gender Smarts, you are now newly equipped to give to and receive from others in a fresh, new way.

Reflect back on this chapter. What will *you* do with what you've learned? How will *you* be different in the next conversation you have? Who will *you* begin relationship-ing with differently?

As you've read these pages, you have focused on boosting your Gender Smarts. Applying them to your relationships starts with *you,* the Common Denominator. As you commit to a BIG Give you will usher in Collaboration boldly.

How the New Equation all Comes Together

The next chapter is the reason I wrote this book. This is where relationships can go from good to amazing. So, here is how *The Art of Relationship-ing* allcomes together:

- *Trust* has to be present for any relationship to have a chance of being great. It is the foundation you build upon.

- *Brainy Truths* expand your Trusting relationships by enabling you to Connect more deeply, easily and more intelligently – brain-to-brain.

- *Gender Smarts* broaden your Trusting relationships by equipping you to Collaborate generously and wisely with greater awareness – gender-to-gender.

- *Partnership* is what you're primed to go for once you have Trust, Brainy Truths and Gender Smarts in motion.

With your new view of what's now possible, it's time to explore Partnership and learn all about the truly WOW! results that transform relationships.

Chapter 6

It's a... Partnership!

"The present is for action – for doing, for becoming, and for growing."

– David Viscott

Partnership doesn't just happen. It's born. It's *your* choice. Partnership is where Connection and Collaboration meet-up and inspire contribution in each partner. Yes, Partnership is the ultimate destination in *The Art of Relationship-ing*.

In this book you have learned new ways to Connect and Collaborate. With them, you will open doors to new relationship possibilities through Partnership. *That* is what this book is all about. You find new simplicity, fulfillment and abundance in relationship-ing this way. And, there's a depth – one I didn't have until a couple of years ago.

Chapter 6 • It's a... Partnership!

As I wrote earlier, I was married for 17 years and then divorced. It was then that I noticed I needed to make some changes in *me*, in hopes of improving many of my relationships. I also had the desire for new relationships that I'd yet to find.

So, my new personal journey began. I started my coaching training and was seeing real differences my new Brainy Truths were making in my personal and professional relationships. At the same time, I also kick-started some personal development work and independent study around Gender Smarts. My knowledge and awareness about Trust and its significance was building in the background.

All of a sudden, this blending started happening. It began in me, and then I carried it into all of my relationships – one-at-a-time. You know what happened? As I showed up differently, I began engaging with people differently. Then my relationships began to sweeten and deepen. They felt more real than before, because they were. I began to establish true and meaningful Partnerships with people and didn't even know it. But, I see it now – how it all came together. The rhythm and flow of this book explains how it all happened for me and how it can happen for you, too.

Recall the equation I set forth at the beginning of the book:

From Trust to Brainy Truths to Gender Smarts, you have seen how the New Equation comes together. All of the pieces are here for you. Your time is now. Partnership is yours for the *choosing* and yours for the *making*.

This book provides *you* – the Common Denominator – the way to bring yourself to relationships so that *you* can begin to see the ripple effect in your life. It's not about changing others or managing results; it's about becoming an upgraded version of *you!*

Chapter 6 • It's a... Partnership!

The Big Shift

There's a major shift that enables Partnership – the shift from compliance to contribution. And, you have discovered the Science and Soul of what fuels that shift. How you Connect brain-to-brain begins the process, and how you Collaborate gender-to-gender completes it.

Let's look at both ends of this spectrum.

Compliance Mindset

Relationships that have a tone of compliance are described as conforming, acquiescing or yielding. "Have to" mode describes them best. Don't be fooled and think, "Oh, no. That doesn't describe the tone of *my* relationships." Chances are that you have at least a touch of it somewhere, so keep reading.

When you have a *compliance* mindset your:

- *focus* is on what's required

- *outlook* is routine and everyday

- *actions* feel like chores, tasks and duties

- *performance* is ordinary, functional, tactical and mediocre

- *results* are run-of-the-mill and commonplace

With compliance, one person "owns" and drives the plan for "us." There is no co-ownership or sharing. The plan "owner" is the solo contributor. Others comply. The results "we" achieve are not "ours" – they are the "owner's" results.

Contribution Mindset

Relationships that have a contribution mindset are described as giving, enriching and sharing. "Want to" mode describes them best. Don't be so fast in thinking you're in the contribution comfort zone already! See this description and honestly assess if it fully describes you – or if you have some room to grow.

When you have a *contribution* mindset your:

- *focus* is on what's possible

- *outlook* is evolving, expanding and engaging

- *actions* feel like opportunities, volunteerism and experiences

- *performance* is innovative, strategic and accomplished

- *results* are extraordinary, satisfying and remarkable

With contribution, "we" co-own, share and create the plan for "us." By our plan and design, "we" are each contributors. The results "we" achieve are "ours."

Contribution requires that you have a plan – for creating a "we" mindset in your relationships (with your spouse, business partner, family, client or team). This commitment to contribution is chosen and led by *you* – and enabled by *your* new awareness around Trust, Brainy Truths and Gender Smarts.

Partnership requires *you* to be both willing and able. Your ability is covered – you've read this book, so you're now equipped. But, it's your choice. It comes from *your* commitment. Like the gradually rising sun, Partnership happens one conversation at a time, not in an instant. You can begin making a shift to contribution with the very next conversation you have.

WOW! Factor

WOW! results are created in Partnership regularly. The extraordinary happens often and is only possible through the contribution and unity of the relationship. Do your relationships WOW!? They do and will when they are Partnerships. WOW! happens when you get the unexpected in a good way.

It reminds me of when I decided to make crème brûlée. I was expecting to open the recipe book, find the recipe, and see its many ingredients and tediously time-consuming instructions. Nope, none of that. Instead, I found that it was made up of just four basic ingredients – cream, sugar, eggs and vanilla. The recipe had simple steps and only took about 15 minutes of preparation before it went into the oven. Easy.

And, mmm-mmm, the final product – that impressive, knock-out, elegant dessert – was a real WOW!

When you create Partnership in your relationships, you will get results that you couldn't have imagined. It's because of the synergy and flow that are produced by *two partners simultaneously contributing* – that's the magic. That's the

Chapter 6 • It's a... Partnership!

WOW! Partnership is attractive, contagious and distinctive in its generosity. Partnership will look good on you.

It's here that partners are enabled to fully *be* in the relationship – head and heart. It's because everyone's contribution is welcomed and wanted. Since we are each designed to contribute and to give of our natural strengths, talents and passions, this place of welcome really feels like home.

In Partnership, we come with a subconscious list of all the things we want to do in and through the relationship. It's all for the purpose of achieving great results together because Partnership is defined by participation and joint interest.

Two people contributing wholly and completely make Partnership happen. Welcome to the world of "want to" in relationships. It is definitely something to WOW! about.

Now, this level of WOW! is hard to understand until you've personally experienced it. Think about New York City. You can hear about it, see pictures and even listen to a recording of the sounds on the street, but you will not really *get* New York City until you've been there. That was my exact experience with Partnership.

Post-divorce, I was establishing newness in myself and my relationships. Years of doing things poorly in relationships taught me a lot about myself. And, I was motivated to start doing things right!

My journey was going well as I studied, learned and experienced much of what I've written in this book. These experiences and truths were all validated by me through study and personal experiences, research, client coaching and team training.

All of the goodness and bounty in relationship results I had pondered, considered, dreamed about and craved – it was happening. It had moved from possibility to reality both personally and professionally. And then it got even better.

The synergy and flow of Partnership were becoming mine with family, friends, colleagues and clients. But something was missing. The one piece of Partnership I craved most – with a romantic partner. I believed it was possible but hadn't created it for myself. That was me for a while.

Then came Patrick.

Patrick is my husband and my Partner. Aside from my relationship with God, Patrick is my life's greatest tipping point. All of the transformation I had created and expanded in my life became enlivened and amplified through my Partnership with him. It was like the wonder of having a black and white TV and then having it come into color. WOW!

Patrick brought new color to my life, as I did his – we were both experiencing true Partnership, in a romantic relationship, for the first time. This was great enough, but there was one other unexpected WOW! – I became a greater, fuller version of myself. Partnership made it happen. Patrick helped me to experience it at an even deeper level and to know and believe in the possibilities.

It All Starts With You

Partnership doesn't just happen; you have to work for it. The first move is *yours* to make. The ball is in your court. The buffet table is filled. What will *you* do with what's before you in this book?

Your choice and *your* intention are required for Partnership. What *you* want to have and create begins with *you*.

Hello – it's just the two of us here, again. So I'm going to bring this back to *you* – the Common Denominator in each of your relationships. I wrote this book for *you* – that *you* would have a clear pathway to Partnership. Every day I wrote, I prayed for guidance that I would write about what would make the greatest impact in your life.

Are *you* willing to make a shift and go for something new?

Years ago, I remember being unsure if this shift was really possible or if it existed only in dreams and movies. But, being dissatisfied, I decided I had little to lose by trying something new. I am glad I did because it led me to a new life filled with the results I most wanted.

And, it can be for you as well. You'll find that when you show up as a Partner in relationships – talking, acting, responding and relating like a Partner – people will respond differently to you. Your world will change, and so will theirs.

So now, you've heard, you've read, you've considered. It's time. You have the possibility and the power to create the ripple effect that leads to radical change in your relationships.

The Art of Relationship-ing is my pathway. It is real. It worked and still works. *Now, it's yours.*

Chapter 6 • It's a... Partnership!

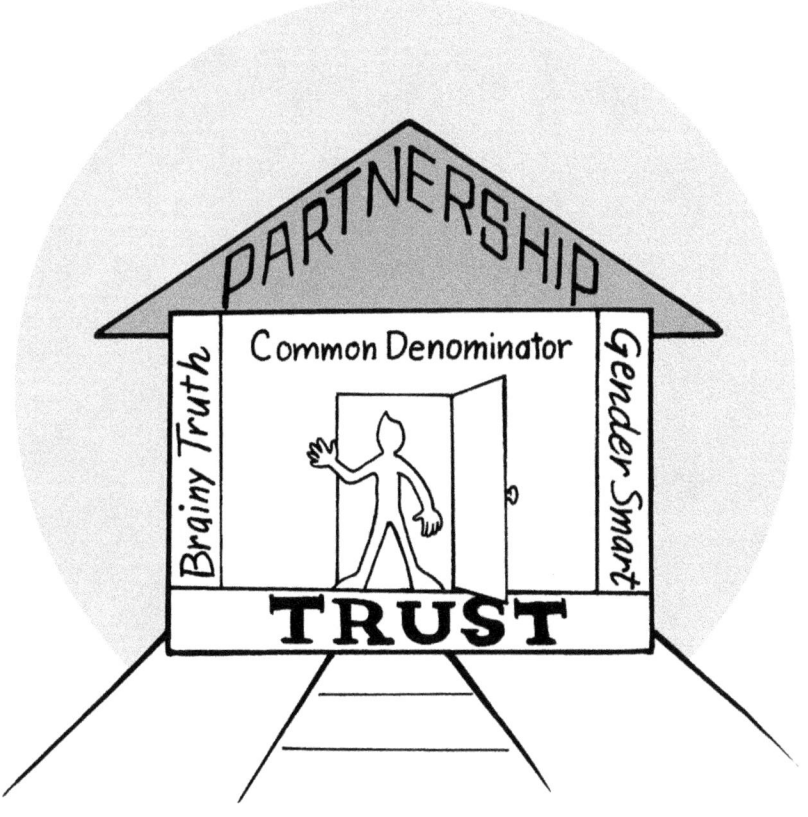

Afterword

The Rest of the Story

"Trust is relying on God to work things out
even if you don't know *where, when, how* or *why*.
It is obeying even when it doesn't make sense.
Instead of trying harder, you trust more."

– Rick Warren
(paraphrase from *The Purpose Driven Life*, Day 10)

The Art of Relationship-ing

In these pages, you've now learned, seen and experienced *The Art of Relationship-ing*. My hope is that you will now take this new information and make it your own – creating the relationships you've always wanted with greater simplicity and fulfillment – while you're being WOWed by their transforming results.

I personally have been WOWed through the writing of this book – in unexpected ways. For me, it has been a faith project; let me explain.

The idea for a book has been bubbling for years. My clients and audiences have been asking for it; the time had come. After a visit with my colleague Christine, I felt newly empowered to put my pen to paper and get to writing.

So, a month passed, and although I was inspired and empowered, I had yet to write a page. Ugh. But, I had started something new, a 40-day study entitled *The Purpose Driven Life*. This book is divided into 40 daily readings. Why 40? Because there are several biblical examples of how God used people for 40 days to bring about significant events and change. Cool – I was all in, and so I started that study. The first nine days were wonderfully renewing for me and my faith.

And, then came day 10.

Afterword • The Rest of the Story

On that day, I was inspired to pick up my pen and follow the prompt I was feeling from God: to set everything else aside and write this book...now. So, I committed to doing this. I saw the book as a way to fully express and share the depth of my work – to give more than I had time to give in my presentations. I was enlivened because the book would be a means to further help people enhance their relationships. Terrific!

I was also compelled to complete the whole process – writing, editing, design and print – before an upcoming trip. So, I looked at my calendar, decided I would start writing the next day and would have the printer start the press right before I left for my trip. Yes, I wanted this to happen. I felt sure that if God gave me the inspiration to do this, that He would also help me make it happen.

About two hours after that decision, I looked back at my calendar. I decided to count the days between when I would start writing and when the printer would start printing. Guess how many days it was? 40 days – WOW!

So, I woke up the next morning and began writing. I also began gathering my '40-day team' – all the people who would say 'yes' to this crazy timeline and commit to it with excellence and heart. One by one, I was connected to just the right people. In their own ways, each of them acknowledged three things: (1) this time line was *crazy*, (2) they would *partner* with me to make it happen, regardless, and (3) they would be *committed* to our work together – in excellence and heart.

And, they did.

Day by day we all worked diligently. And hour by hour my work improved. WOW again. I'd initially thought that the purpose of writing the book was documenting my work. It was, but then it went further – it expanded and deepened the work. I know that was a blessing and an answer to prayer. My intention everyday was to write about what would make the greatest difference for you, my reader. So, when God brought insights to my mind during this 40-day journey, I pondered and incorporated them into the work.

As I continued my personal daily readings of *The Purpose Driven Life*, *The Prayer of Jabez* and *The Message*, I gained new clarity and awareness about my work and my writing – and it improved.

My 40-day team was also filled with amazing energy, inspiration and excellence. I wasn't surprised – we were each under the influence of prayer.

Afterword • The Rest of the Story

The book started with hope and belief – and *my* making the first move. I teamed-up with incredible people who I Connected and Collaborated with beautifully. Together *we* contributed and created. *We* established Partnership. *We* were living *The Art of Relationship-ing,* and for me, I know that it was God who sprinkled His magic dust on each of us to make it happen. And, it did…in 40 days.

About the Author

Laurie Grace Bouldin helps clients and audiences bring simplicity to relationships so they can achieve more of what they want – at home and at work.

What makes her unique is her energetic, positive attitude combined with a message that is unique, relevant, and practical:

> "There's a simpler, more fulfilling way to *relationship* with others that leads to transformed results, both professionally and personally."

Laurie Grace is a graduate of Baylor University, a certified coach through Results Coaching, an ACC credentialed coach through the International Coaching Federation, a licensed Texas CPA and a professional member of the National Speakers Association. She does extensive training and research with PAX Programs, a relationship-focused organization based in California.

She has 17 years of experience in corporate America which provided fertile ground for her research and study on improving relationships through Collaboration and Partnership.

A Texas native, she resides in Dallas with her husband, Patrick, and their two dogs, Riley and Morrow. She is a self-professed lover of great food, red wine, fine stationery, and fountain pens.

For more information on hiring Laurie Grace for your next event, visit www.LaurieGraceBouldin.com.

www.ingramcontent.com/pod-product-compliance
Lightning Source LLC
Chambersburg PA
CBHW050828160426
43192CB00010B/1934